Traction

Traction

Poems

Mary Makofske

The Ashland Poetry Press
Ashland University
Ashland, Ohio 44805

ISBN: 978-0-912592-11-4

LCCN: 2011936766

Cover art: "Release." Carved of Carrara Marble.
Copyright © 2011 by M.J. Anderson, sculptor.

Cover design by Nicholas Fedorchak

Author photo © Gar Wang

ACKNOWLEDGMENTS

The author gratefully acknowledges the publications where some of these poems previously appeared:

Birmingham Poetry Review: "A Child Is Sent for the Globe," "Every Church Should Stand at a Crossroads"
Blue Unicorn: "The Compass of Love"
Calyx: A Journal of Art and Literature by Women: "Bureau of Engraving," "Out of Hate's Country," "Absolving the Myths," "Why I'd Want You at My Deathbed," "Like Peter Rabbit, Whom He Much Admires"
Clackamas Literary Review: "Traction," "Browser, Adult Entertainment Store"
The Cream City Review: "A Personal History of the Early Fifties"
Cumberland Poetry Review: "The Wound-dresser," "The Iceman"
G.W. Review: "The Gardener near Verulamium"
Flint Hills Review: "Reading History beside a River"
Iowa Woman: "Falling"
The Kerf: "Perspective: A Lithograph"
Louisville Review: "Three Elegies for the White Mare"
Lullwater Review: "Dispersal"
Mississippi Review: "At the Recycling Center"
Natural Bridge: "Poem Sprouted on White Ground," "In His Thirty-fourth, Ultimate Summer"
North American Review: "In a Book on Neolithic Wounds"
Poet & Critic: "After the Cold War," "The Facts"
Poetry: "Planting the Meadow," "A Lesson," "Euthanasia: A Geography"
Poetry East: "In an Unnamed Country," "Questions for Solomon"
Quadrant (Australia): "L'Enfant's Avenues," "Those Ruined Photographs," "In a Greek Taverna," "Near Edenville"
Snake Nation Review: "Acoma Pueblo"
Spoon River Poetry Review: "An Inward Bruise"
Whetstone: "Still, Life"
Wordsmith: "From the Window"
Zone 3: "Night of Moving House," "Not Love, Exactly"

"White Gloves" was originally published in the anthology *Tangled Vines,* Second Edition.

The following poems were included in the chapbook *Eating Nasturtiums* (winner of the 1997 Flume Press manuscript competition): "Dispersal," "Falling," "A Personal History of the Early Fifties," "The Compass of Love," "Absolving the Myths," "The Facts," "A Child Is Sent for the Globe," "Facing the Ocean, Wellfleet, Massachusetts," and "White Gloves."

"Dispersal" received the *Lullwater Review Prize*; "Falling" shared first place in the *Iowa Woman* contest; "The Wound-dresser" received the Robert Penn Warren Prize from *Cumberland Poetry Review*; "An Inward Bruise" received the Editors' Prize from *Spoon River Poetry Review*; "At the Recycling Center" was a finalist in the *Mississippi Review* poetry competition.

CONTENTS

I.

In a Book on
Neolithic Wounds

In an Unnamed Country

In her haste to salvage what she could,
some flower vendor must have dropped
this tulip on the pavement near the curb.
Or husband bearing from the florist shop
an anniversary bouquet, as those first
shots were heard, was jostled just enough
to loose one flower, now the only color
after rain has washed away the blood.

The few who slink beside the buildings
will not stoop to lift it. A tulip
can't be eaten, can't be fired. How did
these yellow petals and this fragile throat
escape the heels of panic? It still breathes
as in a meadow, waiting for the bees.

The Gardener near Verulamium

Roses and camellias unlatch their buds
under his expert hands, but one May morning
his spade turns up the unexpected, a seedpod
severed from its bony stem; its empty
eye sockets stare him down. *Bene*, the Roman
says, basking in light for the first time
in ages. He could use a bath, the mosaics
cool beneath the feet he has misplaced
like a pair of old slippers under his earthy
bed. And the gardener, no Hamlet, chides Yorick
for disturbing his morning, balanced on his palm
like a debt. Now he must call the authorities,
and men with tiny picks and whisk brooms
dainty as toothbrushes will sift his garden,
dislodge the roots he's cultivated
over the strata of defeat and conquest.

In a Book on Neolithic Wounds

In an ancient skull
a notch, clean as the ax
blade that struck it, proves
what men may recover from.

The fossil record shows
assault's long history
and motives we can guess:
a neighbor's wrath,
a dispute over a slain
mastodon. Here is the tip
of an arrow lodged
in a rib, yet this ancestor
died of old age, gums spongy,
hardly a tooth left.

What had saved them?
Leaves and roots
they knew, part chemical,
part magic. The chants
they hung their lives on.

Mysterious, the body's own
healing powers, stitching
wounds with scars
and throwing off infection.

Our toughness becomes
mythic. Flesh, nerves, pain
worn off these clean
bones, these hard heads.

The Iceman

In 1991 a mummified body more than 5,000 years old
was discovered in a glacier in the Alps.

He emerges head first, neck bent,
bald as an infant breaking
his mother's waters. Sunlight
cradles the polished skull.
Stunned, he leans his forehead
on his stark reflection.
His shoulder blades protrude
as if he's struggling, pushing out
from his long gestation. His skin
is leathered, dried by glacial air,
an ordinary hunter time has bronzed
to value, like coal pressed to diamonds.

As the foehn retreats, the glacier
draws him back into its blue-lit
womb, and when the rescue comes,
he must be pried from ice
that might have spit him out
in pieces. His worth unrecognized,
he's hauled to lie face down,
nameless and starkly modern
as bodies we have seen emerge
from Auschwitz and Cambodia.
Starved not by human cruelty,
but cold, and time.

His stone ax, bow, and flint-
knapped arrows soon bring down
the world, which views his body
laid in state on a lab table.
While scientists expound, we wonder

at the dried mushrooms, medicinal,
no cure for the storm that killed
him. But mostly, we fall prey
to his physical presence, the chin
that juts like the prow of a ship,
and the left hand open to receive
a gift, perhaps an easy sleep.

The other, desperate as a claw,
might have gripped a wooden handle.
Or is it death the right hand clutches?
The cartilage of the left ear
must have broken; the scalloped shell
is folded forward, as if to block out
sounds long disappeared—his name
called by his fellows, the cry of vultures.

How little it takes to make
the Iceman human, the lid above
his left eye, falling shut as if
caught on the ledge of sleep.
Beneath the skull, an intact brain
locked in its final dream. And though
the blackened tongue that thrusts
against his teeth has forgotten
its language, he must speak,
revealing his age and the food
of his last meal, old injuries
and the illnesses he suffered.
All but the view through those
empty eyes, a vision receding
like the glacier beyond our power.

Absolving the Myths

Domestic Animals Will Not Obey a Menstruating Woman

Oxen shrug off their yokes.
Hens sharpen their beaks and brood
on the young they will not give up.
The dog will not guard or fetch, but gnaws
on the bone of his compromise—
dead meat on the hearth, and fawning.
At her approach sheep scatter,
cows and goats withhold their milk,
the horse will not keep the furrow.
She stirs the memory of crag
and unfenced meadow
where they were herded
only by hunger and weather.
Cats, always licking themselves
clean of orders, narrow
their eyes in approval.

A Menstruating Woman Can Spoil the Food

This change without recipe or rule of law
threatens the mayonnaise, the brewing
beer and cider, cream
that's meant for butter.
Corseted and tied to her tasks,
she leads these small rebellions,
whispering to the shredded cabbage
not *sauerkraut*, but *mold*.
Spreading revolution among the pickles.

A Menstruating Woman Can Cause Impotence

Warriors dripping with blood
of deer and antelope,
your enemies' heads or hair
strapped on your belts
or their deaths notched
on your Howitzers—
If you shrink
from her flow, don't say
her vagina is ringed with teeth.
You could bathe in kill blood
day and night. Is it her fault
you fear the blood of life
on your most precious weapon?

Blades Will Dull If Touched by a Menstruating Woman

Let the pulse of every man and woman
course safe under the tender skin
of the wrist. Let razors be too blunt
to sever the core of a woman's pleasure,
or force her to open herself to a man out of fear.
Let throats no longer be slit by the malice
of thieves, or by their desperation.
Let borders no longer be carved in the flesh
of those they claim to protect,
and the blade no more divide
these fields among neighbors.

Acoma Pueblo

High on a treeless mesa, having paid
to visit the inhabited pueblo, paid again
for the privilege of taking pictures,
we follow our tour guide past
adobe buildings, their glass windows
lit with children's faces
pulled back quickly into shadows.

At each corner stands a woman
with her wares set on a table:
red clay vessels, white bowls
bound with geometrics signifying
rain and thunder, earth and lightning.
I lift one and it breathes
the coolness of a cave against my cheek.

I think of explorers delirious
for gold, whose spirits sank
when Eldorado's shimmer
panned out as the play of light on earth.
Walking the border between pilgrimage
and pillage, we lean to snap
our photos without framing
scarred Ford pick-ups and the empty Coke cans,
outhouses perched on the mesa's edge.
The drinking water of the cistern
looks not fit for bathing.
We were more at home in Bandelier
among the ruins of a vanished tribe,
where we could populate the cliffs with visions.

Inside the mission church
a faded Jesus bleeds while Mary mourns.
Set higher, on the ceiling, the old faith
of earth, sun, moon, gleams on.
A faith still practiced, says our tour guide,
and then turns away our questions.

Outside, we stare up at the mission bell
acquired in trade by some shrewd priest.
His words burn in the quivering air:
>*For this bell, blessed*
>*by His Holiness the Pope,*
>*the King of Spain asks only*
>*ten strong children.*
>*I'll come at dawn tomorrow*
>*to select them.*

We leave the pueblo by the trail
the first priest climbed.
Surely an apocryphal story:
determined to mine their souls,
he labored upward as the rocks they hurled
pierced the armor of his prayers.
At mesa's rim the whole tribe
leapt and screamed, till one child
lost her footing, plunged
from the stained glass sky
to land in the priest's arms,
saving them both.

Still, Life

The poem about the bomb has no
bomb in it. Only a bear scratching
her haunches against a chain-link fence
in the middle of wheat fields ripe
with warnings. Honey drips
from her jaws, she has reamed a hive
this morning, and her breath is sweet
with nectar and bees. She is wrapped
in fat for the long winter, when she sinks
deeper than sleep, not into death,
but into birth. She nuzzles the fence
enclosing the silos, buried missiles
pointing skyward rows of teats.

The poem about the bomb has no
bomb in it. Atomic energy becomes
the power of atoms holding the world
together, intricate bridges of molecules,
allegiances shifting responsive to touch,
to need. Granite, wood, and diamond
swimming through the world that swarms
around us, as we hold ourselves together
for a time at the busy intersections
of the brain, molecules and atoms
driving the traffic of ideas, making nothing
out of something to a great fanfare
of horns and whistles, combustion
of such energy we almost forget
where we are headed, round and
round, neither created nor destroyed,
but, ultimately, in a different form.

After the Cold War

You wake one morning before the alarm, and some burden
has lifted, like a tumor you carried painlessly for years,
discovered by accident on an x-ray, excised before it spread.
Or better yet, benign. The world, and light
slipping in through the shutters, the host
of quarrelsome sparrows outside the window, benign.
For a moment you cannot remember, but you do remember
feeling this way before, a child, with only the ordinary fears.

X-ray. A word that triggers memory's chain reaction.
The bullet-nosed missiles arcing like fireworks, the visible,
and invisible bombardment. Yet it lifts again,
radiating from your body, letting you stretch
into the possibility of war and pestilence, the slow,
or fast, erosion of the atmosphere. Which are,
as a scientist might say, a different order of magnitude
from that glowing fear in the heart. Though it's true
that once you've grown a tumor, you can always
grow one again, you rise from sleep as light as helium.
Eyes burned with revelation, the classic cloud and firestorm
recede, like a dream that wakes you in a cold sweat,
but which you cannot recall as you ease yourself
into the steaming water, or rise to lift a towel from the wall.

Browser, Adult Entertainment Store

A bell alerts the owner
that he's entered, eyes sweeping
the shelves. Easy to jump
to conclusions about why he's there,
both tempted and repelled
by forbidden pleasures and pleasures
he knows so well. The women's bodies
splayed across slick pages
remind him of the flayed
carcasses of traitors, of butcher stalls
where racks of meat, displayed
for sale, attract a chorus of flies.

A woman, skin like cinnamon,
hair black as his wife's, a sheen
that could hold the print
of his hand. When his wife's face
slips over the model's like a veil,
he wants to veil her with a burka,
lowers his gaze when the flaunted
body begins to wear
the face of the woman
his daughter would become
without a father to protect her.

Allahu akbar, the words he holds
under his tongue, sustain him
as he enters the action on a screen,
fits his wife's thighs to the woman
who grips and moans. How can they turn
such intimate moments into scenes
that kill the soul as they inflame
the senses? Sometimes he cannot abide

her silence when he works
his way into her body, or strikes
her when she has obeyed
too slowly, though her dance
like falling water washes over
him now, when he must not
wish for dancing or love songs
seductive as poppies.

        His gaze falls
on a high-heeled sandal, straps
like bindings, the punishing arch
that curves the woman's foot
for his desire. He wants to slip
his fingers between the leather sole
and her skin, touch the scarlet nails
with his tongue. If only he could litter
the streets with these demon shoes,
see women running barefoot,
their soles flashing.

Questions for Solomon

Northern Iraq, 2003

The man brings his story to reporters
because no one else is left to judge.

Tells how the stranger filled his doorway,
cradling the assault gun like a baby,
demanding the return of his ancestral home.

The man waves his deed to the land
like a flag, demanding justice.

One house I built with my own hands,
he tells them. The other, yes, was
there before, and might have been
where the stranger was born.

Who will decide which man
will gain possession, and where
will the other go with all
he possesses tied onto a cart?

Who will allot one house to each family?
What words will these men exchange
as they cross their thresholds?

Who will divide the already meager
fields? What will these fields grow?

Out of Hate's Country

Her sons grow to men
who face all faces
with undamaged eyes,
wait for each soul
to speak its name.

They don't know
what an old country
she's from, how she must
translate in her head
the grace that rolls
from their tongues.

The past spins
a powerful hex.
She hushes pride, spits
over her shoulder for luck.
As much as what she's said
or done, her silence
has kept them safe.

Some moonless night
she will rip out
the words of hate
sewn into her coat
and bury them deep
where all bones embrace.

Reading History beside a River

It's happened so often we know what to expect:
the dictator finally dies and all the prisons are opened,
the army lays down its arms, people sing in the streets,

or the liberating forces march into town while citizens
lean out of windows and line the route cheering and waving
flags of their salvaged nation. Even the city crushed

and burned to ashes finally ceases to smolder. Survivors
have nothing, perhaps not even their sanity, but still
children are born, boxes and metal sheets are pieced

into makeshift houses. Or after the barbarians, homesick,
have left the capital, or adopted the manners of the conquered,
intermarried, forgetting booty and the blood of battle,

water runs clear through the wells again, and merchants
open their doors to the eager crowds. Only optimists
believe the piles of bones will rest, the mountains

of shoes will forget their feet, that no matter how dark
the clouds of smoke from the crematoriums, the dust
will settle, and we will have learned a lesson too stark

to forget. Even cynics must admire our blind persistence,
which begins to look unstoppable, and may concede
that in spite of the worst we do, we can be more forgiving

that anyone might have supposed, more forgiving,
in fact, than the ruined waters of this river
winding its way toward the pitiless sea.

II.

Traction

L'Enfant's Avenues

Washington, D.C., 1960

Driving at night, the first night with the windows
open, under the whispered complaint of leaves—
where were we going?

It didn't matter, along the avenues
from one pool of streetlight to another, girls
with new licenses.

We shared no secrets, only the avenues
too wide for barricades and the desperate
with flaming torches.

We didn't know the roads were designed to yawn,
safe in the minds of our country's fathers.
All fathers worried.

Our gossip was blown out the open windows
to settle like fallout along avenues
where couples ambled.

March meant to parade, *demonstrate* to show
what you meant. We'd never heard the term *civil
disobedience*.

Rounding the flood-lit Capitol, we headed
for Sousa Bridge and our sleeping neighborhoods.
We crossed the river.

So many rivers to cross, the avenues
silent as if waiting. We yawned. We had been
circling all our lives.

A Personal History of the Early Fifties

This was the time before permanent press.
Witness after witness took the Fifth
as my mother unbent the rigid arms
of shirts she'd taken from the freezer. The iron
hissed, smoothing out the creases. McCarthy jabbed
the men and women, grilled them till they were done.

I didn't understand what they had done.
When the Senator took the Army on, TV press
coverage ran all day, while my mother jabbed
pins into skirts and called Joe the Fifth
Horseman, and my father tried to iron
out grievances, shirtsleeves rolled over hairy arms.

I could not imagine the arms
race, or what atomic bombs had done
to Hiroshima and Nagasaki. But the Iron
Curtain fell in school, where teachers repressed
the name of Soviet Russia, and from the fifth
grade's maps every Communist country was jabbed.

Whenever a stubborn employer jabbed
holes in a contract, my father was up in arms,
bewailing the fact that by the century's fifth
decade the promise of the Wobblies was undone,
forgotten, crushed by government. Ike dodged the press,
looked thoughtful on the greens, choosing an iron.

My mother made sandwiches for picket lines, iron
faces few scabs dared to cross, and jabbed
her finger at the evening news. I began to press

for a haircut, tresses long as my arms
weighting me to childhood. Creditors dunned
as my father's sure winners came in fourth or fifth.

Every weekend my parents broke out the fifth
of vodka and proceeded to iron
out the world's problems, deciding who had done
the most for the working man, who had jabbed
him like a heavyweight. I put my head in my arms
and slept, empty of opinions to express.

At the time I felt like a fifth wheel as they jabbed
their way through history, Iron Age to nuclear arms,
though I was the issue, half-done, easing off their press.

Bureau of Engraving

My mother made money
during the War, when men
were scarce and money
had to be made.

The bond tough as fabric
between her thumb and fingers,
woven with colored fibers
to make it distinct,

was sleek and pressed
as clothes fresh from the cleaners,
not dirty yet with the touch
of hunger or greed.

In the Bureau of Engraving
she handled a currency
so fresh it could almost speak.
Enough to make her dizzy,

to dwarf what she already
knew how to make. Outside
the Woodward and Lothrop windows,
she'd marked the fashions,

gone home to cut from the day's
bad news a pattern to copy
dresses she couldn't afford.
Now fortunes of money

lay docile under her fingers.
She brought down the blade

that sliced yard-wide stacks
into bills bound and packed

while the multiplied eyes
of presidents and statesmen
judged her coolly. Singles, fives,
tens, hundreds. After a while

it could have been anything:
pork and spice into sausage,
a nut on a bolt, a uniform.
There was a brother

whose harelip needed mending,
a mother and father gone
to ground, and this routine.
She didn't know the secret

of the ink, she didn't know how
the plates were made, only
the printed fabric she cut
into pieces, knowing

they'd never be shaped
to fit her form. They nicked
her fingers, and she wore
the cuts, still smarting, home.

Traction

One day when I came home from school, I found
my mother sitting in a chair and bound
in a white canvas sling that held her chin
high with a rope on a pulley. *Traction*

she told me as I stared at her perfect
posture—no dowager's hump or long neck
thrust forward now. Tied to this rack, she felt
she had to tell the story: untried, cold

lake and sweltering sun. Egged on by friends,
she toes the boulder. Heat waves rise, she bends
and launches, scribes a perfect dive, descends
into a lake too shallow, into pain.

One moment's recklessness, she said to warn
me, though my sluggish body seemed not born
to follow hers. Because I was as much
in love with her lost youth as she was, such

advice could only gall me, for to dare
was what I wanted, to be like her, care-
less in old photos, vamping on a street
in wartime Washington, her rakish hat

swept down across one eye, like curtained hair
of Veronica Lake. The years before,
she was never skirted, aproned like her
sisters, but leaned against a tractor

or a brother with an ease I envied.
Sometimes she bent her head and made me knead

her neck and shoulders, tendons taut as wires,
not only for the pain, for she could bear

pain, but for pleasure I could give her when
I loathed to give her any other. Then
I blamed her, as the poor begrudge what the rich
have squandered. Fishing on that first date

with my father, she hooked her own bait,
threading slick night crawlers on the hook, not
squeamish like this city man, she thought.
What was there to fear? *She caught a sucker,*

my father said with a laugh when he told
the story, and over the years she stopped
smiling at his pun. Already her heart
was beginning to kick as if wanting out.

When she renounced her youthful daring, I
did nothing to save that fearless diver.
The strap gripped her chin, as a parent holds
a child's face when she needs to be scolded.

White Gloves

In the dim room sour-sweet with fever
      my mother ladled ice cream
            on my burning tongue.

Outside, day melted into night
      and no tomorrow
            could scar me enough

to keep my nails from clawing
      the pox
            erupting on my skin.

My mother brought me
      her good white gloves,
            eased them gently

down around my fingers
      saying, *Now*
            you are a lady.

And I was. Their white gleam
      a shield between my urges
            and my nettlesome body.

Pale sheath of *lady,*
      how you melted
            against those later

fevers, the itch
      of desire. My mother
            dangled her white gloves

before me, but I saw
          her wearing her flesh
                  with ease—

the curves of her feet
          barely contained
                  in her summer sandals.

Dispersal

She sits in a room where the air
brews like weak tea. She must prepare

herself, disperse good china,
silver, the untuned piano,

antique chifforobe and desk
between grown children whose requests

and dropped hints gather on her mind
like burrs, the seeds of argument.

The sepia light now clambers
up her legs into her lap. Where

does it come from? Tinted, she thinks,
by the oak between house and fence

so that she and the room are trapped
as in an ancient photograph.

The children were like light, nothing
she could hold. She wanted to cling

to her possessions. She must let
go. Surely light's this adamant

only through dead leaves reluctant
to fall. Winnowed through spring's green slats,

would it be water chilled with lime?
She marvels that she's never seen

these seasons of light. The dust motes
beautiful, scattering like hope.

Every Church Should Stand at a Crossroads

At a T in the road, where Route 94 heads
east, there's a church so close to the pavement
a slight miscalculation could drive you
right up the concrete stairs and through the wall,
taking the intricate stained glass with you.
If you leave what remains of a chassis
propped on what's left of a pew, the front wheels
softly revolving, you might see how light is
broken coming through the colored puzzles
of tall windows, how it gathers itself again
into one light and disperses, doubly golden,
as when sunlight sifts through sugar maple leaves
in autumn. Organ pipes cup the stillness,
and the scent of wax rises like incense,
redundant on the backs of pews
already polished with the oil of hands.
Brought here by happier accidents,
you might attribute your awe to the vow
that passes between man and woman,
or the name sealed with water to an infant's
head. But it's not true. Belief
was a childhood fever. Which seems
more real, the illness or the cure?

Falling

They bend over the innards of cars,
hands plugged to the sparks of motion.
Or crouch under sinks melting soft wands
of solder to liquid, touching it
to jointed pipes where it is drawn
into the fault to harden against water.
The friends of our son
crack open the door of the future
and enter, tools lined up in boxes,
to fix what is broken.
Bent over his guitar, he too
is concerned with mending.
In his room each day scales soar
into a hymn, the ritual chants of monks
who kneel at dawn in meditation,
and he moves through the visible world
like a man whose faith has already
sworn him in as a citizen of heaven.

But tonight he straightens and begins
to talk of something to fall
back on, the Friday paycheck,
what he can sell for a living.

Amid machines and engines, gears and valves,
bridges, assembly lines, assembly language,
it's easy to assume his hours
of practice are something less
than an apprenticeship.
A calling.

Fall back, the lieutenant cries
to his beaten soldiers.

Fall away, says the demon
that lures us from grace.
Our words, taken in at last,
come out of his mouth.
And sound like heresy, like treason.

A Lesson

At a table in a Jersey restaurant
where we celebrate the upcoming wedding,
the divorce attorney pulls from her purse
a new one hundred dollar bill and holds it
to the light on the wall behind her.
There's something gossipy and familial
about her explanation of how to know
a counterfeit, as if she's revealing
the secret of telling the twins apart.

Echoing his portrait, Franklin's shadow
is easily visible when light
shines through the paper, and yes,
the vertical line as well. What
do the other patrons think of this
revelation, the attorney still twisted
in her chair to hold the bill up
as her voice now assumes a courtroom
tone? What do I think, a woman
of small denominations, not sure
I've ever held a hundred dollar bill?

The attorney's business is making
great matter out of small distinctions,
tallying deceptions and disputed money
that press a wedge between vows,
but tonight she shares this knowledge
gratis, showing the difficult bond
of our currency, its fine markings
that must be so lovingly copied
to a product the innocent will trust.
It may be the wine that makes the whole
enterprise, legal and illegal,

begin to resemble a courtly
waltz. How we depend on each other,
counterfeiters so artful they support
those whose living it is to make
their task impossible.

Night of Moving House

Trucks of rain rumbled across the sky's interstate.
My windshield dissolved and I drove underwater
along the foam of white at the edge of the road.
All right, all right, I shouted, *that's enough—Stop.*
Rain hardened and pelted the glass with ghostly
rocks. Each in our small wheeled boats
navigated the point in the road that always floods,
where pampas grass bowed down the more
I would not, while fists
kept pounding the roof and hood.

What did it want? It wanted nothing. I wanted
too much. To stop driving back and forth
from the old to the new, to settle at last
in the rented rooms and prop the neglected plants
near a light-filled window. One more trip
to check that the doors were locked, everything
cleaned out, but as I pulled in the drive I saw
one maple next to our house had toppled and lay
in the arms of the other. It leaned over the house
and trailed an enormous branch across the shingles.

Lightning flared and the leaves showed black
and shaken. It flashed again, like a cold slap
on my face. *Not now,* I thought, as the soaked tree
shuddered, the bulk of what we owned below
its weight. Because sunlight had sifted through
its leaves of honey, because it feathered with bloom
in April's breeze, it had stood too long peering in
our bedroom window. Now it reached out its arms
for the house we had abandoned. Moving through
rooms with flashlights, we found no damage,
would never have known that death reclined

on the roof. I stripped, ran the last hot water
into the claw-foot tub, and soaked in darkness,
daring the tree to fall, the lightning to come.

The Facts

However we hear of it, the plug and socket of sex,
the piston of generation, the bearer of tidings
must become alternately god and traitor,
and the silence that cupped us all those years
more traitorous yet, our ignorance
a pratfall we performed again and again.
Our bodies, tuned to leap and race,
destined to stumble, break the rules
of every game we've fenced the world in.
Our will a fragile seedling, but the root
feathered and clawed and driven as those flocks
swerving as one creature, following seasons north or south.

For a while the public world is penetrated
by the private: clothes lift like fog from couples
on the street; our parents, our kindest aunts and uncles,
shuttered away, do messy, unspeakable things.
Sex spied through a keyhole, afflicting someone else.
Until, insinuating as a cat, the facts
wind round our ankles, and curl purring in our laps.
And so in time we face our children, their faces
shining up at us for answers. Given
the facts, they reinvent the mystery:

Why do you do sex? What is it for?
They do not mean survival of the species;
we do not mean the scratch that soothes an itch.
How to explain that flight from flesh
on fleshy wings? Even as they long
for breasts and blood, or the first jet of semen
waking them from dreams, we know how often
they hug their fickle bodies, and murmur as if
to a lover, *don't change, don't change.*

Children, we want to say, you are not lost.
You can learn again to be your bodies.
We would never be spirits except as bodies.

III.

The Uniform of Flesh

The Wound-Dresser

Open doors of time! Open hospital doors!
                                        —Walt Whitman

1.

Who calls me from the grass I know so well
to lead me down the streets of Mannahatta
as the soil of the grave falls from my shimmering atoms?
A chorus of voices raised, not in song, but keening,
another great rift in the Union of soul and body,
another fierce war dividing brother from brother.

What are these corridors pristine as galleries,
these quarantine warnings and cautious attendants?
Fearless I enter the rooms of the dying.
I examine the tubes and monitors of anguish.
Would you measure a man's pain with dials and needles?
Would you bind a man's pulse and breath to a chart?
Let me look in his eyes, I will give you the figures.
My hand on his cheek will calibrate his fever.

2.

Oh rusted body! Flesh corroded from the lath of bones!
Do you believe this young man is demented?
His eyes do not wander, they follow me as I drift about the room.
Yet his glance ricochets from the other who sits the deathwatch,
the love on his face like an open wound.
Skillful as a surgeon, I open the patient's life, his history and future.

Are these the young men I sought under the gaslights?
The ones tipping back their chairs in the corner of a Bowery tavern?
Is the city I dreamed spread out below us?

3.

In the Village a cabaret singer plays to an almost empty bar.
Waiters stand outside cafes, wiping their hands on their aprons.
Yet I see this avenue is lit with ghosts, my comrades, who fill the
        streets of Mannahatta,
and lean over the rail of the boat, squinting for the sight of Fire
        Island through the fog.
They crowd the streets of San Francisco, and jostle through the
        narrow lanes of Provincetown.

And they still meet behind the volunteer fire companies,
and on the high school football fields after the lights are out.

Must I change my triumphant songs?
Must I indeed learn to chant the cold dirges of the baffled?

4.

The preacher rises on his toes behind the pulpit.
He means to change blood into wine, intoxicant that clouds
        the senses.
He means to transform flesh to bread, stale crumbs scattered in
        the wilderness.
He tells his congregation: A bullet hovers in mid-air.
First only a speck in the distance,
it could be a hummingbird whose furious wings hold it steady as
        it unrolls its tongue in the deepest flower.
How long it is barely visible, a bird on the horizon of sight, a mote
        of dust that floats on the cornea.
Larger it grows, so gradually larger until its direction is clear,
till it loses wings and brilliant colors and desire for sweetness,
gleams silver and intent, its trajectory veering as the sinner veers.
Faithful bloodhound, casting through woods and alleys, across
        highways and rivers,

its nose pointing always toward the target, it gleams, silver and
          purposeful.

5.

My sons and daughters, there is no cure for death, and the only
          vaccine is love.
You must take it into your veins, the live virus.
Chants of the flesh, chants of the blood and semen, song of the life
          thrust, still will I sing you.
Comrades and lovers by the thousand!
Be not dishearten'd, affection shall solve the problems of freedom yet.
Those who love each other shall become invincible.

(Keep on, my sinewy voice, my muscled rhythms, as the weary
          swimmer is washed out on the tide,
each one of the drowning tangled in his beard.
We must not speak our secret. I am an old man with no answers.)

6.

All night the convenience store glows.
What do the men and women need, shuffling down these aisles at
          two in the morning?
Coffee, car oil, the bread of life, a microwave sweet, a sweet wave
          of love.
I follow a short bald man with owlish glasses, a froth of beard like
          my own.
Moving his lips, he leans over the freezer—
I swear he is saying the lines of a poem,
his hand poised over the steaming ice has grasped an image.
He looks up and almost sees me, peers through his lenses.
He smiles at the young man edging toward him, unsure of
          introductions,

but the look itself is an introduction, and the poem can wait, the
          young man is true inspiration.
I want to grasp the poet by the arm, demand that he revise his text.
I want to take the young man with me into the pure love of
          comrades,
the hand on the shoulder, the intercourse of eyes and words.
But the memory of flesh revives, the kindled body refuses to blaze
          up in cerebral smoke.

7.

Over the sandy arm of Long Island, wind-borne as a cloud,
I remember the gee and haw of muscle and tendon,
the sting of breath in the pumping lungs—
Oh Flesh! Ruddy and sweating, piston legs racing beside the waves,
heart churning tides of blood, oxygen hurtling into every cell.
On a hill lie two young men—Oh comrades!
How the blades of your love must pierce me! How long have I
          been spirit?
Even in life I took off my flesh to love as if removing a garment.
I was made of words, and stroked words only, the spume of my
          cock was words,
and my tongue not made of flesh, as are your tongues on each
          other's bodies.

8.

How I greeted this war with drum-taps and marches, defending the
          indissoluble Union of soul and body.
The corseted waist of each woman would be free, the smooth
          thighs and shoulders,
and every man walk proudly, bearing his body like a medal.
The love of male and female, the love of comrades, would leap
          candid and undisguised.

Every cause shrinks before its casualties.
Only after the heat of battle do we hear the moans,
the cries to God, to Mother—not to Progress, Justice, Freedom.
We have no bandages, we have not planned how to carry them
        away, the soldiers broken and twisted.
We can barely count them, for we had not reckoned the terrible
        toll, the cost.

9.

No more the world en masse, the view from a distance.
As I pass down the aisles of the wounded, they reach out their
        hands—
infants, young men and women, the gray-haired matriarchs and
        patriarchs all know me,
they know I bring no harm, no accusation.
I will tend their scabrous wounds and listen to prayers and curses
        with equal patience.
Theories and creeds burn off in the heat of their dying.
May all sermons and parades and exhortations, including my own,
        now crumble to ashes.
And you there, beyond these hospital walls, do not forget those
        who precede you into death.
On earth there are no civilians. All wear the uniform of flesh.

The Compass of Love

Love sometimes would contemplate, sometimes do.
                                    —*John Donne*

He blazed like a lamp beside her bed.
While in her side a tumor like a sea
anemone grew and fluttered, his hands
steadied china teacups, blue chicory
plucked from beside the woodpile and staked
in a white vase, long-lived even when
cut, chosen over the flashy, tender
roses. He was no man strung out like
wash and flapping in the wind. He knew
things could be learned. As he remembered
that first log propped up to split,
the heavy maul, his muscles bunched
and waiting for a sign how to begin.
Turn and turn it as he did, the wood
said nothing, the maul eyed his legs
wrapped carelessly in denim, his boots
made only of skin. There was nothing
for it but to swing, slice the blue sky
open, aim the wedge of metal at the heart
of wood, and hear the *chok* of tight grain
split from grain. And soon the routine
of the work fit snug as blinders on his fear.

His wife burned like dry kindling
on the bed, and whenever she woke to pain
as if to light, he carried away
what her body did not need and brought
what it did. His face weathered,
his skin a tent struck by the winds
of loss, or so they thought. Grief

can be prodigal; he would give it nothing
more to spend. When she slept he spoke aloud
leukemia, until it seemed the name
of some rare woodland flower
at home in the stream of his blood.
What kind of man, undertakers
whispered among themselves, chooses a coffin
lining as if for a dress? *To match
her eyes*. And for himself, the same.

In His Thirty-fourth, Ultimate Summer

The children he cannot see
build a fortress around him.
A girl, a younger boy, voices
chirping like the wings
of crickets rubbing together:
Moat. Towers. Walls
to keep the monsters
out. Sand hisses
off their shovels. They grunt
as they haul water in their pails.

Ribcage, hipbones, spine
carve his shape in the low canvas chair
he thinks he resembles: remnant
hung on a rickety frame,
dragged over the beach, set down.

Somewhere past the breakers'
alternating threat and apology,
his wife lifts her feet from the sea floor
and rides the swells, looking out
for the next wave, and in
to the tableau of her family.

He is amazed how much he knows
of this, memory standing in for sight,
and clues he can build on.
In sapphire blue, gulls swivel
on rusty hinges. Domed clouds
when the heat on his skin
suddenly cools. Down the beach
lifeguards attract a static
of voices. Brine spiking the air

deposits a thin crust on his body.
Under the straw hat, his face feels shadowed.

Summers along this shore
ride toward him like waves.
He recalls the path they meant to take
along a spit of sand that tapers off
to nothing. A walk for low tide only.
Once at sunset they tried it
too late, water sniffing their heels
as they made their retreat.

Now his children have thought
of another game. *Lie still*,
they say, and already filled
with the emptiness shores demand,
he dozes, wakes only when he hears
a bubble of silence explode
around him, and he knows
he should shake it off,
but he likes the weight and heat
that press him now.
He cannot help his wife
above him, trembling,
jeweled with water,
her face frightening the children
who've tried so hard to bury him.

Fox Stole

They died for beauty
they could not perceive,
her lovely shoulders,
her hair's matching glint.

Inside the curtained
alcove near my bed
they circled, teeth to
tail, with lidless eyes

the sleep I hunted,
terrified to catch.
My mother soothed,
my father brought the light.

Shy as a fox, I
could not name my fear—
those weeping bodies
rising from their lair.

Why I'd Want You at My Deathbed

Because you'd curse
death, then make
a joke about it.

Because you'd bring
a stack of papers
you must grade
but not grade me.

Because you have the faith
I lack, and would not
preach it.

Because you'll later find me
in a sign—a white crow
or a shattered glass.

You'll know it's only
in your mind, but
where else would I be.

Euthanasia: A Geography

Spoken, it looms
like some vast island
he did not mean
to discover.

Its rock wall spans
the clear horizon,
daring him to scale
cliffs without footholds
to the bleached plateau,
treeless, cracked by heat.
Beneath a molten sky
spined bushes hunker.

The landscape he might
have mapped takes his own
measure. Now he must shoulder
light and shadow, chiseled
sky, and let the stars
draw closer.

He scans the distance
for the way across,
the pass through mountains
he does not choose to name,
words precious as water.

Consumed with thirst,
he walks in circles
till the land that seemed
too stark for bones
dissolves in sudden rain.

White blossoms open, fall
from clots of berries
poisonous, but sweet.
And what he thought were stones
unfold their wings.

IV.

An Inward Bruise

An Inward Bruise

...the sovereign'st thing on earth
Was parmacetti for an inward bruise.
*   —Henry IV, Part I, quoted in Moby Dick*

What does the whale do with so massive a brain?
*   —Carl Sagan*

1. Photograph: Faeroe Islands

Whale skulls and vertebrae
jut from a berm where a fisherman
leans on the island handiwork.
The bones are laid in parallel
lines, a skeleton for the wall
that divides the fields.

Holes where nerve chords ran,
eye sockets, and the ivory hulls
that shielded what whales know
are packed with earth.

2. The Schism

Buried deep beneath the fat
that insulates them
lie nubs of bone, a pelvis,
all that remain of hind limbs.

An experienced crew can flense a whale
an hour, yet how difficult to strip
from the language of evolution
all judgment, choice. They turned
away from land.

Chance after chance
building like deltas at the mouths
of rivers. For some, air beckons
with trees, wind, roiling weather.
For some, the clasp of water,
mountain ranges never lit by sun.

The vaulted arches the whale
builds toward the infinite
are bone and flesh,
obscuring the curious
eye behind the jaw.

3. Scrimshaw

Engraved with a fine tool, this tooth
is honed to art, a scene at once
accurate and abstract. A whaling ship,
its sails and rigging carefully rendered,
spawns longboats bristling with oars
and sailors. The sea lies dead calm—
only a few lines, level, propping up
the boats. A sperm whale spouts an inverse
teardrop not unlike the bubbles netting
words in comics, but the whale's is empty
except for blood, which does not show
in this brown and white sketch, muted
as the whale's sight, we believe, though always
we are wrong about so much. A harpoon strung
to a taut rope protrudes from its back,
while a sailor, leaning forward as if
resisting a wind, brandishes a gaff
as he strides along the whale's head.
Perspective is not the artist's skill:
another whale swims above the horizon

60

and with a flick of its tail severs
a boat that pursues it through the air.
Over this scene enormous birds, even larger
than the whales, hover for spoils,
though their wings and legs are locked
in postures of crucifixion, and they do not
seem to be flying, but falling.

4. Devilfish

In San Ignacio Lagoon the gray whales rise
to scrape against the keels loose skin
that flakes off like the memory
of whaling. Devilfish, the sailors
used to call them, for they were vicious
in their attacks, the cows especially,
defending their young.

Protected for decades, they loll
in these tropical waters, circling
boats and tilting one eye
toward tourists that line the rails.
It seems a compromise, this voyeur
industry, and we think it was our idea,
though the whales approached us first,
cruising near boats like envoys
waiting for recognition.

5. Mythology

Dionysus, fearing treachery from sailors,
hurled them into the sea and changed
them to dolphins, incapable of doing harm.
The Greeks revered the dolphin,

the friendly whale that folklore claims
can save the drowning. On an ancient coin
a boy rides a dolphin docile as a horse.

In the mythology of sharks
the dolphin cuts a darker figure,
a ramming iron whose force
can detonate a shark's internal organs.

6. The Study of Dolphins

The Navy considers the applications.
Espionage. Defense.

What the dolphin asks
is answered by echoes that tell
not only the shape of an object,
but its composition. Iron, copper,
plastic, steel: what humans form
and form again in words.

Blindfolded dolphins can read
an object's thickness and density,
and choose the one we request.

They're not reliable, though,
for planting explosives
on enemy ships, for some
return and latch their payload
to the ship they've left.

In the tank their keepers
are more than shadowy outlines.
Unlike sight, sound penetrates
to bone and lung. What enters water

dolphins know through and through.
Hunger, heart rate, quickened breath:
the raw materials of need, love, fear.

7. The Search for Extraterrestrial Intelligence

So lonely on this watery planet,
we probe the skies with radio signals,
hoping for life that can speak
in translatable language
or in the cool tones of mathematics.

Surely others exist in that garden of stars.
Speculation often draws them like us,
two-legged, upright. Their hairless bodies
smaller, muscles atrophied, strength centered
in the brain that swells the cranium,
their heads like giant seed pods
on too frail a stem. Their music
a charm that could win our trust.

8. Whalesong

Humpbacks flood their ranges with songs
we could call haunting. Scientists
frown. Emotion's a territory
claimed by the human species.

Yet more than science
responds to unearthly cries
repeated and embellished,
floating through the easy medium
of water, through wooden hulls of boats
steered by fishermen and warriors.

Sirens, they called these singers
who lured them over the edge.

9. Patterns of Culture

A diver rolls over the edge
of the catamaran. His wetsuit
clings tight as skin, dark back
and white belly, legs encased
in a sheath that ends in flippers
joined to mimic a fluke.

His arms are wrapped to conceal
the nimble thumbs and fingers
that have grasped the world
and turned it to his purposes.

His purpose now is to swim
without the alternate motion his legs
know from walking land, to arc
his body along its length and glide
as the dolphins teach him.
The meaning of gestures
may differ from culture to culture.
When the dolphins defecate
around him, he hopes it is a sign
of welcome.

10. Regarding Each Other

Displayed together on a table,
the dolphin brain and human brain
regard each other like fighters
in the same class. Fighting—

so human a metaphor,
so much of our brain devoted
to weapons and competition,
to housing theories
or our vulnerable bodies.

And what engages the convoluted
cortex of the dolphin? Maps
of oceans, language? Knowledge
of self? Of death?
When we mimic their voices,
what are we saying?

Like lovers, we reach through darkness
for each other's bodies
in search of the mind's light.

11. Those Who Swim with Wild Dolphins

Hour on hour they spin and dive
embraced by water, synchronizing
their movements with the dolphins'
until they swim beyond the physical
into an aquamarine of trance.
They swear time loses meaning,
fear drops away in the joy
of submersion, dance. Around them
dolphins glide and mate, chatter
and eye the curious intruders
streaking their portraits
through the water's colors, composing
a visual language with breath
that floats in quivering globes
to the surface. All they create
disappears, leaving no trace

an archeologist could follow.
Not only touch vibrates
with meaning; the spirals they weave
echo the helix where life began.
The swimmers drift far from the boat
till fatigue or cold forces them in.
Coming aboard again, they often weep.

12. The Belly of the Whale

You were the maw that could swallow
ships, the dark unknown that rimmed
our flat and narrow world.
A mystery sunk in our hearts
that could devour us.

Now you lie in your niche
of order, family, species,
diagramed and studied.
We were never your prey,
and only when you were ours
did your body become a weapon.
What have we to fear?

Lone dolphins that seek out
humans may become possessive,
sometimes pushing a favorite
far from shore. Stroking and play
may lead to roughness. From the genital flaps
emerges a phallus, serpentine and red.

On both sides, desire
to understand intensifies,
and mystery demands some myth.

13. The Study of Humans

Sick and disoriented, a young sperm whale
lies moored in a New York harbor.
The distress it pulses out can stun.
A man on the dock feels its force
beneath him, and when he places his hand
on the creature's head,
its calls make a tuning fork
of his fragile bones.

Off the coast of Australia a pregnant woman
lowers her taut belly into water.
One by one the dolphins approach,
bowing and clicking to scan her torso,
and we've watched on hospital screens
the image they hear: curled body
with its heavy head, fingers bunched in fists,
eyes closed, gills healed, lungs folded
tight as buds. The cord throbs with currents,
mooring the fetus in its salty bay.
The clicks of the dolphins grow rapid
as gossip. They bring their infants
into the shallows, the danger zone.

14. Water Music

On his sailboat a man plays
an oboe, and from the glassy water
a whale rises on its flukes,
then submerges and arcs
its great body above the surface
like a note held almost beyond endurance.

To be so created
that your motion through the world
caused so little turbulence,
to be sheathed in skin
pliant as the element around it,
what would neurons spark
across the synapses,
if you did not need
to move mountains, but only
to be them?

V.

Not Love, Exactly

Not Love, Exactly

You can't say to your child
"Evolution loves you."
　　　　—Stephen Dunn

Some mornings the world you rise to shimmers
with such a preternatural glow, you're afraid
you've wakened in some alternate dimension.
Nothing makes sense, not the crisp angles
of streets and houses, not grass, trees, sky
(why blue, not green?). The squat dog lifting
its leg at the fire hydrant regards you
through white bangs, making you question
what could have framed so inexplicable
a creature. We could be breathing deeply
and sighing, *Ah, that fresh ammonia,*
or taking a brisk morning shower in
hydrochloric acid. You've been lost
often enough to know how far one missed
turn can take you. It could all have come
to something quite different, or to nothing,
anything but lilac blossoms woozy
with fragrance, your own irrelevant wonder.

Landscape, with Memory

Imagine a child imagining
out of her pain a landscape:
a path around a lake, bridges
arched over a web of streams.

Willows sun-braided and trees
iced with bloom. Two porcelain
swans, rising from sequined
water to eat from her hand.

Imagine a woman waking
to the dream. The harsh laugh
of ducks and alarm of geese,
their droppings on the path,

a can, discarded, bobbing
near the shore, the algae bloom
fade into backdrop, yield
a clutch of willows sifting sun.

Reflections of reflections.
Has she been here before?
It grows again into her
thought, that ideal landscape.

Not real, and yet her real
life rushed to fill it, shaped
to its contours. As if, standing
on a bank—earth the margin

from which green sprang
up and down, twin clouds,
twin flocks of birds—she had
stepped out and walked across the sky.

A Child Is Sent for the Globe

She rose, and though the boundaries
of the world were blurred through eyes
that would need glasses in a year,
it was not sight that failed her, but
the word. She scanned the room,
and every nameless gimcrack grinned
and reared. Lumps of glass that broke
light into rainbows. Metal jaws
that made a pencil whirl in perfect
circles on her paper. The black disk
edged with holes, for piping notes
before they hung their voices there.
In the ring of children she had
left, laughter strained at the cage
of decorum. Above the racks of books,
propped on a stand, a ball—bright,
mottled, rough. She passed her hands
above it like a conjurer, and hearing
her classmates' indrawn breath, moved
on, as if anything she touched,
if it weren't true, would burn.
Before the teacher, seeing she was lost,
came to her rescue, even the children
at their desks had raised their heads, until
the whole class followed her aimless ramble
in search of a world beyond her grasp.

Perspective: A Lithograph

At the top, beneath a strip
of sky, some blowsy clouds,
one bare tree scarcely larger
than a thimble stands
beside a solitary house
and field of grain the wind
leans on. Small strokes
of clothing, puffed out
by the breeze, dry on a line.

A pastoral scene, except
this world we recognize
clings like a beetle
on the apex of a pyramid.
The soil that roots the grain
lies sheer as skin, gravel and clay
beneath, two narrow bands.
Strips of shale, then bedrock,
not solid as its name
but cracked and split,
the percolating water nested
in pockets, seeking its own level,
being sought, the well
for the house sunk deep
below ground's rim.

Beyond the plumb of the well,
layer on layer descends
to the burning center,
though of course the scale's
distorted, no frame

large enough to hold
the depth of earth
beneath the world we know.

Facing the Ocean, Wellfleet, Massachusetts

A real estate so little real
dunes migrate on the roads
and nothing is ours, no more
than bluefish wall their plot of ocean
or gulls claim territories on the waves.
The deed that was not witnessed by the sea
is a plucked feather, a shell
pricked by an oyster drill.

What deep words can describe
the pastures of their fathers,
their fathers' horses, heads down,
tethered to the grass, ambling
along Billingsgate Island, now
a sandbar rising from the waves
only at low tide? Lawns, gates, fences,
the tower that proclaimed the land
melt like salt in the wavering light
where fish explore the roads of memory.

We walk this strand
between whatever comes next
and the glacier that beheaded
mountains, ground the stones
to grain, and built the skeleton
of all the Outer Lands—
long moraines that run like backbones
from which hang the grassy marshes
and the plains of sand, and pods
of water sprung from underground.

Each winter's sea prunes back
this shore, each spring the waves
lay down another beach.
Where we stand
is the closest we'll come
to walking on water.

Like Peter Rabbit, Whom He Much Admires

My grandson fits inside the hollow,
head pressed against its roof,
legs tucked inside the cage of roots.

As if the pine has cast a spell to calm
his shouts, the gallop that propelled
him past the shore of Dyer Pond

this morning of late summer, too cold
to swim, too cold to wade in after frogs,
he grows so quiet, touching bark

as if his hands could speak, the tree
could listen. We speak in whispers
of the dangers he's escaped,

his love of hiding, all the warnings
we have given when his feet have flown
him far beyond our sight and voices.

Cradled and snug, he presses ear to earth,
sap dripping on his hair to leave
a kiss so firm we cannot wash it out.

From the Window

In the snow ideograms
where birds have walked
recording their hunger.

Flakes from a sky of ashes
cover the broken husks of seeds.

Two small yews we planted
live through their first winter
beside a pine stump in the shadow
of a sapling, its trunk girded
by another winter's need.

At last our neighbor has removed
the baskets brimming with red
plastic flowers, like lewd gestures
in this pencil sketch of lake and trees.

Near Edenville

Stone fences ring the fields where cows still graze
and cornfields, stubble now, gleaned by the birds.

New fences laid by masons show that time
and the proper tools can shape a wall precise

as mathematics. Old ones that farmers
made to clear these splinters from the glaciers

were balanced with rough skill and the mortar
of resentment. Rocks came up like weeds,

despite how many they had cleared away.
No point in wasting anything. The makeshift

walls meant no post holes to dig, no split rails
to string. The old walls run along the roads

until they sink, like streams gone underground
to bubble up a little further on.

And some, like soldiers going from attention
to at ease, are sleeping scattered in the fields.

With nothing to protect, they can become
themselves again, and not what they were trained

a while to be. Bluestem gone wild seeps over
empty lots. Walnuts, cedars, maples, oaks

sprout up past raspberries and Jimson weed,
field mustard, Queen Anne's lace, and chicory.

In barns packed to the rafters with baled hay,
steaming with the breath and body heat of cows,

cats slink in search of mice and breed so well
only cars that speed along the narrow roads

can thin them out. More and more the barns
begin to lean, and one curled shingle pried

up by the wind tears free. Like the building
of consensus, one board torquing, then

another three, the rusted nails yank loose
till it unmakes itself without the plan

construction took. I've never seen it happen,
but one day the barn is there, though twisted

as if some giant hand had wanted to
unscrew it like a lid, and by the next day

it's collapsed to fill its shadow. Only
the beams are left, and can be sold, like land

going to the highest bidder. They grace
cathedral ceilings and look down on china,

crystal, Oriental rugs in new homes faced
with fake veneer to match the native strain.

High-market masons resurrect the fallen
fences, shearing the rounded stones to make

them fit like puzzles, making sure they're level.
Craftsmen allowed to take their good, sweet time.

Those Ruined Photographs

Think of the photographs we called ruined:
focused on a scene we meant to capture,
sawgrass cutting against a gunmetal
sky, or the almost vertical mountains
circled by switchbacks we couldn't believe
we'd maneuvered. How we framed the vista
with tree trunk or boulder, near object
to anchor the distance that flowed away.
So intent we never saw our shadows
enter the scenery we longed to keep.
And what odd silhouettes we make, inky
brands that prove our ownership. Our bent arms
raised as if to funnel songs into our ears
or cup our mouths and call the landscape in.

In a Greek Taverna

Food here is layered as civilizations.
Phyllo leaves stacked and mortared
with butter, crisp and gold as leaves
that fall now, but much thinner,
more like leaves of the Bible, or some other
text brittle with age and study. Underneath
lies spinach, green as spring that waits
under autumn's leaves, and under every text
we have devised. See how more phyllo,
changed by what's come after, appears
again at the bottom of this excavation,
as war or peace, or wind or water's
vengeance cycles through our lives.

Spanakopita, moussaka, souvlaki—
not only history's vast sweep, but
kitchen time, the cook who's sweating
by the stove and with such patience
builds these gastronomic monuments
that disappear in hours, only to rise again,
a phoenix from the fire. Nothing
is singular, everything's a tribe,
skewer packed shoulder to shoulder,
lamb, eggplant, pepper, and dolmades'
sacred leaves wrapped and sealed,
keeping their rice and lamb
cryptic as Delphic prophecies.

How should I end? With baklava,
more sediments of time
dense with nuts and honey?
Ingredients the same as those
first stolen from trees and hives

whose rings and cells we copy
in what we shape to feed
both appetite and art.

At the Recycling Center

Next door at the Humane Society
the dogs are barking. Our town has made
a New York channel with the story:
dogs confiscated from an owner
who now wants them back. The trial's dragged on
for months, and till it's settled, the dogs
can't be adopted by new owners.

Hauling a plastic bag of trash, I climb
the rickety metal stairs to the landing,
upend the bag and shake its contents
into the open hatch of the paper
and catalog trailer, larger than my
kitchen, almost full. Sliding down the hill
of paper is the last Sears catalog,
which I was tempted to save. As long as
they kept coming, they were of no value,
but last things appreciate. It's Tuesday,
I'm the only one here, so I can linger
gazing down into that huge bin of
correspondence. A sheaf of bright coupons
catches my eye, as it is made to do,
and redeems a lost word: *rotogravure.*
The surprising rhyme for *you're* in "Easter
Parade." Today the rotary press itself
is obsolete, like the name the process
gave to the newspaper supplement.
Now the remembered lines of the song
yield Easter bonnets and the parade,
which survives as a parody of itself.
At least the sonnet has not disappeared.

I've crumpled or shredded to confetti
receipts with our VISA number

and ripped into quarters even unclaimed
student papers, so no one can reuse
their words. Though each semester
"from the beginning of time" and "let us
hope in the future" keep creeping back.

This heap is so high I can still read
the lists I've discarded—house repairs,
friends invited to the party and dishes
they'll bring. Paint back porch stairs,
wash windows, prune roses, take recycling,
and here I am a month later, one more
item to check off the new list at home.
I wonder if we should reuse the same list:
do laundry, check car, get groceries,
and the grocery lists, too, which resemble
variations on a theme.

                    Afraid to leave
evidence of our lives within easy reach,
I push our trash out toward the edges.
This exposes someone else's recycling,
an unfamiliar script, and leaves of notebook
paper, a child's homework. The blue lines
filled with textbook letters remind me
of our sons' first printing and the merge of
letters into cursive, leaning into
a distinctive style. This bin must be run
through with such laborious practice,
the alphabet we need for this volume
of words. Beyond the homework lies a pack
of letters tied with a faded ribbon.
Tradition dictates what they are, yet who
would discard them whole? Burning's preferred,
both thorough and symbolic. What is dead?
Both lovers? Love? And who decided
they should end at this communal site?

Less and less needs to be hoarded, as it
all comes back, though sometimes in another
form, like those stymied poems I've shredded
and discarded. Up through recycled paper
old words rise in new configurations,
as even now the stars are shifting
Cassiopeia and Orion. And here
a postcard shows no earthly destination,
but a huge full moon. I need not
turn it over to know its news. Always
waxing and waning, its white face
making the dogs lift their muzzles and howl
for a new master, any one.

Poem Sprouted on White Ground

When I plant my hands in earth
I want my mind there, too,
inarticulate as a slug,
reading only the scrawl
of bindweed, purslane, on the beds.
Unwinding the circular thinking
of pot-bound roots, I part
their tangles, fan them in loose soil
and tuck around them layers
of the *Times*, knowing its disasters
will by next year soften
into nurture, green.

Here are the remains, just
recognizable, of what we cycle
through this garden: half-rotted
hay and blackened, sour leaves,
and nested in the orange rinds
a clutch of broken shells,
as if the birds had hatched and flown
past these decaying trunks
of kale and Brussels sprouts,
winging through loam toward sky.

Swallows scythe the blue,
but I am sunk in earth
up to my elbows. A locust
bristles in the chestnut tree.
The sun lies heavy as a sleeping cat
across my shoulders. Kneeling
puts me face to face with blossoms
whose colors flare
as I forget their names.

But there's no end to being
what we are. Uprooting words,
I plow their seeds to the surface.
Dusted with pollen, the mind
backs out of the flower.

Three Elegies for the White Mare

Buried in the far pasture, the white mare
I used to pass as I walked.
No matter how I called or whistled,
she seldom looked up.

The snow melts and the grass grows long
in the field where the mare grazed.
After the birds and leaves have gone,
my neighbor finds a nest
lined with a riddle in its hollow
of fine, dark twigs:

white coil of hair
from her mare's tail.

The woman carries the nest
inside, sets it near her drawings,
sculptures of shells, wings, bones.

For weeks she lives with the nest
that recalls the tail flicking flies,
twitch of flesh beneath the curry brush.
And on her palm, the inquiring lips.

One day with pencil and paper
twig by twig she weaves a nest.
Strand by strand she braids the hair.
She props the nest she has made
beside the other.

I carry the images home:
coil of white hair, artist, drawing, nest,
mare I never rode, or even touched.

How long inside its shell
the poem stirs and changes,
then taps its way out.

Still, the absence we pass in the field
will not look up.

Planting the Meadow

I leave the formal garden of schedules
where hours hedge me, clip the errant sprigs
of thought, and day after day, a boxwood
topiary hunt chases a green fox
never caught. No voice calls me to order
as I enter a dream of meadow, kneel
to earth and, moving east to west, second
the motion only of the sun. I plant
frail seedlings in the unplowed field, trusting
the wildness hidden in their hearts. Spring light
sprawls across false indigo and hyssop,
daisies, flax. Clouds form, dissolve, withhold
or promise rain. In time, outside of time,
the unkempt afternoons fill up with flowers.

The Richard Snyder Publication Series

This book is the 14th in a series honoring the memory of Richard Snyder (1925-1986), poet, fiction writer, playwright and longtime professor of English at Ashland University. Snyder served for fifteen years as English Department chair, and was co-founder (in 1969) and co-editor of the Ashland Poetry Press. He was also co-founder of the Creative Writing major at the school, one of the first on the undergraduate level in the country. In selecting the manuscript for this book, the editors kept in mind Snyder's tenacious dedication to craftsmanship and thematic integrity.

Editor Deborah Fleming screened for the 2010 contest, and David Wojahn judged.

Snyder Award Winners:
1997: Wendy Battin for *Little Apocalypse*
1998: David Ray for *Demons in the Diner*
1999: Philip Brady for *Weal*
2000: Jan Lee Ande for *Instructions for Walking on Water*
2001: Corrinne Clegg Hales for *Separate Escapes*
2002: Carol Barrett for *Calling in the Bones*
2003: Vern Rutsala for *The Moment's Equation*
2004: Christine Gelineau for *Remorseless Loyalty*
2005: Benjamin S. Grossberg for *Underwater Lengths in a Single Breath*
2006: Lorna Knowles Blake for *Permanent Address*
2007: Helen Pruitt Wallace for *Shimming the Glass House*
2008: Marc J. Sheehan for *Vengeful Hymns*
2009: Jason Schneiderman for *Striking Surface*
2010: Mary Makofske for *Traction*